# How To Become A Journalist

## Stephen Wilcox

# Liability Disclaimer

By reading this book, you assume all risks associated with using the advice given below, with a full understanding that you, solely, are responsible for anything that may occur as a result of putting this information into action in any way, and regardless of your interpretation of the advice.

You further agree that our company cannot be held responsible in any way for the success or failure of your business as a result of the information presented in this book. It is your responsibility to conduct your own due diligence regarding the safe and successful operation of your business if you intend to apply any of our information in any way to your business operations.

# Terms of Use

You are given a non-transferable, "personal use" license to this book. You cannot distribute it or share it with other individuals.

Also, there are no resale rights or private label rights granted when purchasing this book. In other words, it's for your own personal use only.

# How To Become A Journalist

# Contents

# What is a Journalist

The media industry could not survive without journalists, which means that all who work within the media need some kind of journalism background. Nevertheless, there is a great deal of writing involved in the trade. How much writing depends upon what outlet the journalist is working for: the Internet, television, radio, newspapers, magazines, etc.

Nevertheless, the typical journalist is one that reports the news. It is important to have a love for writing and for what is happening in the world. A journalist must also be as unbiased as possible with a desire to find the facts rather than write based upon assumption.

There are journalists that travel the world and there are those that remain within their hometowns reporting for local newspapers, magazines, radio stations, and news stations.

# Education and Qualifications

The road to becoming a journalist starts with education. It is preferable that you acquire a degree in Communications or English. Those that become journalists without a degree tend to work for small publications and community newspapers.

If your dream is to work for a large publication, you will need to have the college degree to back you up. Keep in mind that the person with the education will land the job before the person who doesn't. This can ring true with smaller publications as well.

A good way to get the education you need is to attend journalism school, which is referred to as "J-School." Don't fall for the shortcut programs that state they will give you a certificate of completion that will help you land the job that you want and need. You should also be wary of those online colleges that state they can accelerate your degree completion because of your life experience. Many of these programs are not affiliated with any university, thus they are not accredited.

Yes, there are a number of quality online colleges that are sister schools to actual bricks and mortar schools. However, you do want to seek out a school with a reputable television program or newspaper. A school that manages its own programs and publications is one that takes journalism seriously. Having as much hands-on experience can also help you land the internship that you want that can help you earn better job placement when the time comes.

As for job placement, attending the right J-school also means being able to take advantage of job placement services after graduation. This, in addition to internships, can help you get past the hurdle that many companies put in front of you before even considering you for employment and that is for you to have experience before you work for them. It is very difficult to get experience if no one will hire you, so you need all of the hands-on experience you can possibly gain.

Your salary will also increase with the amount of education you have. Someone entering a job with a bachelor's degree is going to pull in more money than someone with an associate's degree. If you have a bachelor's degree, you can expect that most employers will be able to meet your salary expectations.

Graduates with master's degrees are those that will have better odds of obtaining jobs. This is because master's programs put an emphasis on advanced research, investigative journalism, leadership and theory. There are also some master's programs that specialize in public policy, investigative reporting, and online journalism. How to report on religious subjects, the utilization of quantitative research methods, and reporting on national security are some of the areas covered.

## Other Qualifications

It is a requirement that a journalist be able to express ideas clearly. Writing should also be enjoyable. The ability to concentrate and work under pressure should also not be an issue. The pressure is going to be felt, but it should not be discouraging. The publisher has a deadline to meet and it is up to the journalist to meet that deadline.

Journalists must also exercise good judgment on what to cover and what not to cover, as well as what to write and what not to write. The idea is to give the public something entertaining and/or engaging to read. When an individual turns to an article or they watch a news broadcast, they are looking for information. All of the questions they are asking should be answered in that story.

In addition, there is an increasing need for journalists with knowledge of graphics, publishing, web design, and multimedia production. Many times, work has to be wirelessly transmitted via email through a computer or wireless device. Online publication requires knowledge of editing tools and the ability to combine the text with graphics, video, audio, and even animation.

## How to Advance

Journalists typically advance in their field by building a reputation, getting published in prestigious publications and markets, and taking on complex assignments. Meeting deadlines will lead to the more prestigious jobs and assignments. For beginner writers, writing on a freelance basis helps establish a reputation. Freelancing also allows beginners to start working as soon as possible rather than applying again and again for staff positions. Being able to show a by-line to a potential employer can increase the odds of becoming employed.

# Internships

Prospective employers love to see applicants that have been interns. This is because an intern has done the job or at least seen it done.

Interns are hardly ever paid for the work that they do because being an intern means doing the job in order to learn how to do it and to get the hands-on experience that employers require.

Interns typically work during college rather than after. There are times in which the college will convert the time spent as an intern into credits toward graduation. And while many do the job for free, some do get paid a small amount.

As for where you can intern, it is up to the field you want to go into. Newspapers, magazines, news stations, and all media fields allow for interns to work within their walls, but not every person looking for an internship with a specific news outlet is going to get the job. There is an application process.

When applying for an internship, you have to prove that you have an edge over the other applicants. You have to explain why you would make a good intern and provide any other information that is requested by the employer so that they can determine who the good candidates are to work with them.

It is possible for a media outlet to base their decision upon a person's background, the school they go to, or the region they live in.

As for the areas you can intern in. You can intern in:

- Reporting
- Blogging
- Photojournalism
- Copy editing
- Designing
- As a multimedia producer
- As a production assistant.

Summer is the most popular season to intern, although many media outlets will allow for interns to work any time during the year. Some internships are part-time and others may be full-time. Some jobs may also last weeks, while others may last months.

When applying, it is very important to apply as early as allowed and to apply often if you do not immediately receive the position. Sometimes the competition is very fierce and the applications are due months before the media outlet makes a decision.

# Jobs in Journalism

There are many different types of jobs available in journalism and they are going to determine salary and a number of other factors. In order to remain motivated in doing your job, you will need to pick your specialty and stick with it.

## Newspaper Reporters

A newspaper reporter covers the news within communities, metropolitan areas, or on a national level. Stories usually break very fast, so you have to be flexible and fast at writing a factual story. Deadlines are usually tight.

## Investigative Reporters

This type of reporter is employed by television networks, magazines, newspapers, and even online publications. It is very important to be able to tell the difference between fact and fiction and to get to the bottom of a scandal, a political situation, or a crime. Research is also very important since this is a "no fluff" job. Accuracy is the key.

## Photojournalists

Photojournalists stand behind the still camera or the video camera to capture images of news happening. These individuals are employed by newspapers, magazines, news stations, and online publications. An artistic eye is required to catch the right moments to record on film. Photojournalists must identify the right moments to be present in order to catch history on film. This means being at the star-studded award show or being in an area where major conflict is occurring.

## Foreign Correspondents

A foreign correspondent reports in countries other than their own. There are many foreign correspondents covering what is occurring in war torn countries, following the military on missions in order to report on them, and much more. Government, religious, and political unrest tends to be the areas covered and that means the job is a dangerous one. Of course, the pay is going to be quite satisfactory, but a lot of travel is involved as well.

## Broadcast Journalists

The television and radio reporters that you enjoy hearing and seeing report the news to you every day are broadcast journalists. They exist on a local and national level. The specialty here is "straight reporting," which means the stories are short and to the point rather than in-depth. Reporting and researching skills are a must, as well as having a pleasant voice and a pleasant appearance. Not usually thought about in broadcast journalism are those that utilize documentaries to delve deeper into a story.

## Sports Journalists

A sports journalist's job is to cover the sports on radio, TV, and in newspapers. Sports reporting requires knowledge of the different types of sports and also requires being very specific about player names and information without a lengthy explanation. These individuals are able to look at a clip of a play and recite everything that is happening in that play without missing a beat. Of course, this is done in writing and, in the case of television reporting, is read back to the viewing audience. Nevertheless, the sports reporter has to know how to write about sports in a way the public understands.

## Online Journalists

An online journalist has to be very fast in reporting the news, which means paying very close attention to events that are occurring. These are individuals that report any time 24/7 and usually do so through online-only publications or their own blogs that have gained a following due to their quick wit and ability to report news fast.

## Editors

An editor's job is to edit and proofread the work that is written by journalists. Of course, this does not mean that a journalist is allowed to make excessive grammatical areas. Editors give the document a second look, fixing it so that it makes sense to the reader. It can be difficult for an individual to proofread their own work because they are so close to it. Editors may also alter the layout of an article and check facts.

# Work Environment

The work environment has changed for a lot of journalists due to advancements in electronic communications. Many journalists are able to work from home or split their time between home and office. In fact, many media outlets enjoy the fact that their journalists can work from home because they do not have to facilitate a work environment for them in-office. Thanks to email, stories can be sent to the editor instantaneously.

There are many writers working on a freelance basis, which means they are paid per assignment. This also means working out of a home office during times that are convenient for them. This also means being willing to work evenings, weekends, and even holidays to meet a deadline.

While many working on a freelance basis enjoy being able to choose the hours they work, there is the struggle of juggling more than one project at a time and the burden of also ensuring the work flow is continuous. This can create a certain degree of stress.

Factor in the fact that many at-home journalists have families and they find that they are juggling family responsibility as well. There is no separation between work and home like there is when going to work at the office. Freelancers can create their own hours as long as the deadline is reached, which can mean working strange hours and experiencing fatigue as a result of so much responsibility occurring in one location.

Nonetheless, the work environment is dependent upon the type of journalism work that is done. Newsrooms tend to be fast-paced with the editor needing the work to be completed as soon as possible. Newsrooms are also not quiet environments, so a person needs to be able to work around a lot of noise and distractions. Broadcast journalists may have their private offices to prepare, but any outlet in which news is breaking is not a calm one.

## Job Duties

Journalists tend to be busy in that it is a must to attend activities and events. You should not be afraid to try and push ahead of the crowd of journalists and ask questions. You must also listen to the questions asked by other reporters and take notes. You have to have a good eye, a good ear, and must be a fast note taker.

You must also be able to document the facts through photo, audio, and video. If you want to be a commentator or a columnist, you will need to offer opinions to your readers. Expect very strange work hours and assignments given to you under tight deadlines.

In some cases, you may be required to travel. Local publications usually do not have this requirement, but medium-sized to large publications and networks will if they cover news on a national level or even an international one.

Once you have gathered the information you need to create a story, you will need to piece together your notes. You will also have to do your own research in order to fill in any gaps in the story.

## Things to do and not do

If you want to be a journalist, then there are some things that you will need to do for yourself in addition to any education and training that you acquire. Those things include:

Even when experiencing down time, you will need to work. Even when you fail, you have to pick yourself up and keep going.

Textbooks will teach you so much, but your true experience comes from the things that you teach yourself. You will need to focus on the area of journalism that you want to do. The standard college courses teach the basics, but certain sectors within the media may have their own special requirements. So it is ideal to look to online tutorials and talk to people willing to give you the answers you are looking for.

You may need to work for free in order to learn how the trade truly works and to gather some experience. Writing for free can help you build the portfolio you need to acquire the paid work that you need.

Before you ever enter the field of journalism, ensure you have a passion for it. This goes back to working for free and talking to others. Becoming burnt out on what you are doing is not the way to become a success.

Network in person and online. Twitter is a great way to find interesting stories to cover, but it is not the only way. You have to keep your eyes and your ears open to find that perfect reporting opportunity.

If you have difficulty finding a journalism job, you can pitch ideas to publications. Learn how to query properly and you could very well sell your ideas.

You will need to keep your eyes peeled when looking for the facts to include in your written pieces. Unfortunately, a lot of information on the Internet is not fact and this causes an issue in reporting. Usually, incorrect information leads to a correction at a later date and this can harm credibility. Always make sure you obtain information from more than one source when possible and, if you cannot find more than one, directly contact the person who provided the information in the first place.

Make yourself visible online by creating a Facebook account, a Twitter account, a Tumblr account, and even starting a blog. You may even wish to start your own website that highlights your work.

Call yourself a journalist rather than an aspiring journalist. This will help you feel like you are a journalist rather than "trying" to become one.

You will most likely create your own set of standards that you will wish to stick to. Think about how far you will go in a story. You also have to consider what you want to be paid for what you have to do.

One thing you will find that you have to do is make your own rules. This means doing what you have to do to put yourself in the right place at the right time. Of course, this is something you will do legally and tastefully. For instance, it is not ideal to use a motorcycle or moped to chase down a celebrity.

You also want to always think outside of the box. You will need to come up with creative ways to get the story you want to cover or to get the job you want. The ability to create strategies and put them into action is very important in journalism because there will always be someone trying to undercut you. Sometimes that individual may work at another news outlet and other times it can happen on your own turf because someone else within the same company may want to land the big story.

The following are the things that you should not do when you are working toward becoming a journalist:

Don't expect to become rich. This is a profession that relies primarily on passion with the potential to make more money in the future. How much you make depends upon how aggressive you are, the area of journalism you work in, and who you work for.

While the profession does go beyond the basics of journalism, it is always good to know the basics well and revisit them when needed.

Don't expect people to step up and help you without you asking. Opportunities don't create themselves.

Do everything you can to not burn bridges. You don't want to embark on a very lucrative opportunity to then fail in a way that the damage is irreparable or you can never use that experience on your resume.

If you're afraid of criticism and rejection, then journalism is not for you. Both of these happen all of the time and should be used as learning experiences in order to reduce the number of rejections in the future.

Don't forget that everything you do on the Internet can be seen. This means you may want to restrain yourself when you want to write that rant in your blog about the newspaper publisher's attitude. You may find that that attitude will tell you to find work elsewhere. Prospective employers and those offering journalism gigs use the Internet as a part of the application process.

Don't tell yourself that you will get started in six months or a year. If you want to become a journalist, you have to start right now because the field is a competitive one.

Overall, there is a great deal of self-discipline involved when you want to become a journalist. You will have to work alone with minimal supervision in some instances, so you will need to minimize the distractions and do what you need to do. You also need to consider that you may have to write about subjects you don't care about. You may also have to work at a very fast pace and this can be discouraging.

## Job Prospects

Competition for journalism jobs is high due to the fact many outlets have converted to online only platforms. The U.S. Bureau of Labor Statistics predicts a decrease of 6% for reporters, correspondents, and news analysts. The moderate decline in employment was predicted to occur between 2008 and 2018.

The good news, however, is that many of the jobs are going to those individuals with new media skills. Because the Internet is becoming a very important aspect of the media, those with the reporting skills, the writing skills, and knowledge of how to use the Internet to release the news are preferred over those with "old school" knowledge.

If you have the education, the hands-on experience through internships or college publications and productions, and you highlight your abilities, you increase your chances of acquiring the journalism job you want.

To become even more employable, study different writing styles and read a lot. You may also want to learn a foreign language. Learning a foreign language means being able to write in that language. This can become very useful if you are working in an area with a population of individuals that do not speak English or you are working in a foreign country. Foreign correspondents tend to benefit well from learning different languages.

## Salary

The salary of a journalist is going to vary based upon the specialty area, degree of education, and the employer. Nevertheless, the salary range looks like this:

- Small newspaper reporters can expect $20,000 to $30,000 annually. Medium-sized papers pay an average of $35,000 to $55,000, while large newspapers pay upward of $60,000. Editors earn a little more.

- Broadcast journalists make between $22,601 and 101,623 per year.

- Sports reporters make between $20,261 and $72,833 annually.

- Foreign correspondents make between $28,597 and $101,063 per year.

- Investigative reporters make between $30,252 and $104,000 per year.

- Photojournalists make between $20,870 and $54,889 per year.

- Editors make between $23,634 and $71,286 for newspaper editors, $18,791 and $107,235 for editors in chief, and between $27,437 and $62,221 for copy editors.

- The salaries for online journalists can vary. The average is $22,146 to $78,241 annually. However, this can be higher or lower if the journalist is operating his or her own blog or media site.

The following is to give you an idea of what some of the most popular newspapers pay their employees on a weekly basis:

**New York Times** – Reporters and copy editors make $1777 per week.

**Providence Journal** – Reporters make $1245 and copy editors make $1297.50.

**Pittsburgh Post-Gazette** – Reporters make $1100 and copy editors make $1115.

**Lexington Herald-Leader Daily** – Reporters and copy editors make $685.

TV reporters tend to make the same amount of money newspaper reporters make when starting out. The bigger the market, however, the more money that is made. Nonetheless, a journalist must work in a smaller market before being able to break into larger markets. Almost all of your national reporters started out at local stations. These individuals, if working in big cities, could make six figure incomes. Reporters in national media markets can make upward of $1 million per year.

# Become a Blogging Journalist

There are some journalists that start their own online operations. There is very little risk involved in this, but in a profession that is very competitive.

The way to become successful covering your own news is to market, market, and market some more. You have to tell people that you are there. As for how you get your income, you need to sell ad space or become an affiliate that markets for other companies through your news blog and hope you make a healthy commission from the ads being there or that the amount of money you sell ad space for is sufficient enough to support you.

Nevertheless, you have to be fast when news breaks because you don't want your article to be old news by the time people read it. In order to compensate for any delays, however, offering commentary or your opinion can strike a great deal of interest in what it is you are offering the public. People tend to like controversial opinions and commentary. If you can offer that, you can build a reputation. Know, however, that doing so takes time.

# How to Build your Reputation

Even if you decide to not blog exclusively, you may still want to utilize a blog to show your more human side. Many times, readers will look at the by-line on a story and want to learn about the person who wrote it. If you are expressing opinions, people want to know why you think the way that you do.

To promote your blog and your position in the media as a journalist, you will need to create social networking accounts. Facebook and Twitter are great places to start. Facebook allows you to create a page and encourage people to "like" it. The more likes you have, the better. Twitter allows you to acquire followers. You do this by following others and interacting with them.

No matter which social networks you choose, you will need to ensure that you keep them updated frequently. On Facebook, you will want to post a status daily. As a journalist, you will want to post something regarding breaking news and include a link to your article if one is available. You can conduct polls and even comment on what is happening in the news. The idea is to keep the public updated on what is happening in the news and to keep them aware of you by posting status updates that will appear on their news feeds.

The same principle that exists with Facebook also exists with Twitter. Twitter is called "micro blogging" and it involves making posts that are no longer than a certain number of characters. You can post what you think of breaking news, links to your stories, and much more. You want to build a solid

Internet fan base and you can post more than once a day on Twitter without annoying your followers.

Linked In is another popular social networking website that works differently than Facebook and Twitter. Linked In allows you to connect with others, while also serving as an online resume. You can connect with individuals you have worked with in the past, while connecting with new individuals. If someone sees your work experience on Linked In, they may present you with a lucrative employment opportunity.

The fourth most popular social network is Tumblr in that it allows you to post text updates, links, and videos. It is similar to blogging with a "status update" twist to it. This can allow you to connect with an entirely different audience.

Finally, you will want to create a website for yourself. If you do not know how to build basic websites, you can pay someone to do so for you. You want your website to look nice, but you can pay someone to put together a simple website without breaking the bank.

In your website, it is ideal to include a bio, links to your work, links to blogs you own, and anything relevant to you. You are more or less branding yourself since you're not selling a physical product. What you are selling as a journalist is your words. Selling your words means people are going to buy your thoughts.

# Ready to Become a Journalist

Now that you know what kind of education you have to have, the experience required, and what the job and salary outlooks are like, are you ready to jump into this fast-paced field?

Yes, the more education the better. You also want to make sure you have the right personality and the right motivation to do the job. You also need to make sure you take advantage of internships that may be available to you. If you find that one internship is too short and you need more experience, apply for another one. You cannot engage in too many internship opportunities because that means more hands-on experience for you and that will look excellent on your resume.

You also have to ask yourself if you are ready to experience criticism from the public. If you cover a story on a topic that makes them mad, don't take offense. You wrote the story; you didn't create the event that prompted it. However, there will be times that you express your opinion that people won't like it. Simply respect their views more than they respect yours and you can move on.

And remember that you will need to brand yourself. When it is your words and ideas that are being marketed, it is important that you become known for your articles rather than your articles be known for you. Let people know who is behind the articles. When they remember that a human being is behind the construction of articles, news broadcasts, and photos, they will relate more.

When you have all of these things together, you have the tools and the motivation to be a powerful journalist. You can work for the small publication throughout your entire career or you can work hard toward working for a national or international outlet that will pay you what you are worth.

# Resources

The following is a list of online resources related to the journalist profession.

## Career

http://mediacareers.about.com/od/mediajobprofiles/a/Journalist.htm

http://www.howtodothings.com/careers/a2730-how-to-become-a-journalist.html

http://sustainablejournalism.org/future-of-journalism/how-become-journalist-tips-from-jschool-grad

http://journalism.about.com/od/careersinjournalism/a/salaries.htm

http://www.bbc.co.uk/journalism/about-us/training-for-journalists/

http://www.beajournalist.talktalk.net/

## Salary

http://www.payscale.com/research/US/Job=Sports_Reporter/Salary

http://www.payscale.com/research/US/Job=News_Analyst%2c_Reporter_or_Correspondent/Salary http://www.payscale.com/research/US/Job=Journalist%2c_Bro adcast/Salary

http://www.payscale.com/research/US/Job=Investigative_Repo rter/Salary

http://www.payscale.com/research/US/Job=Photojournalist/Ho urly_Rate

http://www.payscale.com/research/US/Job=Newspaper_Editor/ Salary

http://www.payscale.com/research/US/Job=Editor_in_Chief%2 c_Newspaper/Salary

http://www.payscale.com/research/US/Job=Editor_in_Chief%2 c_Newspaper/Salary

## Education

http://degreedirectory.org/articles/Journalist_Career_Summary _Job_Outlook_and_Education_Requirements.html

http://www.bls.gov/oco/ocos320.htm

http://cubreporters.org/internships.html

http://www.forbes.com/sites/susannahbreslin/2011/06/28/how- to-be-a-journalist-in-2011/

http://www.sean.co.uk/a/journalism/careers.shtm

7229684R00023

Printed in Great Britain
by Amazon.co.uk, Ltd.,
Marston Gate.